# BYGONE DAYS

# BYGONE DAYS

## Illustrations, stories and poems from years gone by

SELECTED BY

*Leonard de Vries*

CHANCELLOR
PRESS

First published 1984 by
The Hamlyn Publishing Group Limited.

This edition published 2002 by Chancellor Press,
an imprint of Bounty Books, a division of
Octopus Publishing Group Ltd,
2-4 Heron Quays, London E14 4JP



ISBN 0 7537 0720 9

Printed in Dubai

# INTRODUCTION

Books were not produced especially for children until the middle of the 18th century – about three hunderd years after the mass production of books was made possible by Gutenberg's invention of moveable type.

In those three centuries children could read popular versions of classical fables, medieval romances and, later, fairy tales. There were books of instruction – but those were not real children's books in the definition of F. J. Harvey Darton, author of the unsurpassed standard work *Children's Books in England:* 'printed works produced ostensibly to give children spontaneous pleasure, and not primarily to teach them, nor solely to make them good, nor to keep them *profitably* quiet.'

England was the country in which books primarily designed to give children 'spontaneous pleasure' first appeared. The English philosopher John Locke was largely responsible for the change in attitudes which encouraged this development. In *Some Thoughts Concerning Education,* published 1693, Locke declared: 'Children should be treated as rational creatures... They should be allowed liberties and freedom suitable to their ages... They must not be hindered from being children, nor from playing and doing as children... Curiosity is but an appetite after knowledge, the instrument nature has provided to remove ignorance.' These revolutionary ideas were slowly but surely accepted and led to the birth of children's literature.

A new era in education and literature began when the London bookseller John Newbery published, in 1744, *A Little Pretty Pocketbook,* 'intended for the Instruction and Amusement of Little Master Tommy and Pretty Miss Polly' and later *The History of Little Goody Two-Shoes.* The success of these and other early children's books was enormous. Soon other countries, especially Holland, Germany and France, followed the English example. Rousseau's book *Emile ou de l'éducation* (1762) greatly expanded Locke's ideas and furthered the attitude that children were not little adults, but beings with special needs of their own.

I have compiled from early English and Dutch six anthologies of children's books. This volume, *Bygone Days,* is a selection of what I believe will most appeal to children today. It contains several of the finest examples of very early children's books including *Little Rhymes for Little Folks* (J. Harris, London, 1823); *The Alphabet of Goody Two-Shoes* (J. Harris, London c. 1820); *Whittington and his Cat* (J. Harris, London, c. 1825); and *The Talking Bird, or Dame Trudge and her Parrot* (J. Harris, London, 1808). All the colour pictures in the previously mentioned books are copper engravings, coloured by hand. Poor children earned money by doing this.

All the other illustrations in colour in this volume are the result of chromo-lithography, a printing technique using stones – six to ten different stones for each picture and each colour prepared, not photographically, but by hand! Beautiful examples of this chromo-lithography are *The Dogs' Dinner-Party* (G. Routledge, London c. 1870) and *The History of the Four Mice* (Dutch, c. 1870).

Many colour illustrations in *Bygone Days* are from popular Victorian children's magazines such as *Chatterbox, Little Wide-Awake* and *The Child's Companion.* The book also contains many Dutch variations on Heinrich Hoffmann's *Struwwelpeter* (first English edition 1848) – one of the best known children's books in the world, which has appeared in dozens of languages. Examples of the work of Kate Greenaway, the most famous of all English children's book illustrators, are included: *Little Ann and other Poems* (G. Routledge, London, c. 1833), as well as an extract from one of the most beautiful Victorian children's books – *Abroad,* illustrated by Thomas Crane and Ellen E. Houghton (Marcus Ward, London, c. 1882).

Unfortunately, most of the authors and illustrators of early children's books are unknown because they were not credited on the title pages. It is sad to think that they, the creators of these lovely books, were apparently not important enough to be mentioned. Exceptions are *Sing-Song* by Christina Georgina Rossetti (G. Routledge, London, 1872), illustrated in a very pure pre-Raphaelite style by Arthur Hughes, and *Songs for little People* by Norman Gale (A. Constable, WestMinster, 1896), superbly illustrated in an art-nouveau style by Helen Stratton.

*Bygone Days* contains the most attractive pictures I found amongst thousands of early children's books I leafed through in the *Renier Collection* at the Victoria & Albert Museum in London, in the famous *Osborne Collection* of the Toronto Public Library, Canada, and in the rich collections of the Royal Library in The Hague and the Amsterdam University Library in the Netherlands. I sincerely hope that many children, and their parents, enjoy this selection from early children's books, which were made with so much devotion and craftmanship, and that it makes them love these dear old things as much as I do.

Amsterdam, 9th February 1984

LEONARD DE VRIES

# CONTENTS

Some full-page colour plates and black and white illustrations are taken from the children's magazines: VOOR DE KINDERKAMER, CHATTERBOX, THE CHILD'S COMPANION, THE CHILDREN'S FRIEND, THE CHILDREN'S TREASURY, THE INFANTS' MAGAZINE and LITTLE WIDE-AWAKE.

# LITTLE RHYMES for LITTLE FOLKS

### THE DOG TRIM

There was once a nice little dog, Trim,
Who ne'er had ill temper or whim;
He could sit up and dance,
Could run, skip, and prance–
Who would not like little dog Trim?

### THE LITTLE LAMBS

Those dear little lambs, how pretty they look,
All drinking the water down at the brook;
Good bye, pretty lambs! there, now go to play,
We'll see you again on some other day.

### LITTLE FANNY

So, Fanny, my love
You've a pretty new frock,
I wish you your health, dear, to wear it;
'Tis so very neat,
And it fits you so well,
You'll be careful, I hope, not to tear it.

### THE WINDMILL

Blow, wind, blow; and go, mill, go,
That the miller may grind his corn;
That the baker may take it
And into rolls make it,
And send us some hot in the morn.

### THE LITTLE DONKEY

I'm a poor little Donkey,
And work very hard,
To my sighs and fatigues
Master pays no regard;
Yet for him would I toil,
And do always my best,
Would he speak to me kindly,
And give me some rest.

### FANNY AND HER CAT

Come here, little Puss,
And I'll make you quite smart,
You shall wear this gold chain,
And I'll wear this fine heart;
And when we are drest,
My dear Aunty shall see
Who then will look best,
Little Pussy or me!

## LITTLE PUSS

As Pussy sat upon the step,
Taking the nice fresh air,
A neighbour's little dog came by,
Ah, Pussy, are you there?
Good morning, Mistress Pussy Cat,
Come, tell me how you do?
Quite well, I thank you, Puss replied:
Now tell me how are you?

## THE COCK

The Cock crows in the morn
To tell us to rise,
And that he who lies late
Will never be wise:
For heavy and stupid,
He can't learn his book,
So long as he lives
Like a Dunce he must look.

## LITTLE FREDDY

Here comes little Fred,
In his pretty new clothes,
Little trowsers and boots,
And nice little white hose;
His frock's thrown aside,
Now he'll do all he can
To be good and be clever,
And grow up a man.

## THE ROCKING HORSE

When Charles has done reading
His book every day,
He goes out with his hoop
In the garden to play;
Or, his whip in his hand,
Quickly mounts up across,
And then gallops away
On his fine Rocking horse.

## A PLEASANT RIDE

As the weather is fine,
I will take a nice ride,
And Martha and Fanny
Shall sit by my side:
We'll drive by the sea,
And enjoy the fresh air,
Then walk to the pier,
And see who is there.

## A PLEASANT WALK

In the sweet month of May,
When the fields look so green,
Little lambs skip and play,
And nice flowers can be seen;
Then the sun shines so bright,
And the days are so long,
And the dear little birds
Charm the groves with their song.

# Naughty Kitten

# A visitor for tea

Good afternoon, My Lady. Do please stay to tea.
But who are these two youngsters you have brought for me to see?
It's safe for them to play if you put them at your feet.
My two are there already, but you – please have a seat.
We are having lovely weather, you really must agree,
And would you like one lump of sugar in your cup of tea?
But sad to say, our hostess had forgotten one small thing,
And soon she heard, with horror, the teapot's empty ring.
So milk was on the menu, and with sugar lumps as well,
They both thought it delicious as I'm sure you all can tell!

# The Dogs' Dinner-Party

Mr. Blenheim was a very gentlemanly dog, and Mrs. Blenheim was quite the lady; both were well-bred, handsome, and fond of good company. They lived in a nice house, near Hyde Park Corner. One day Mr. Blenheim was in the library, dozing in his armchair after dinner, when Mrs. B. thus addressed him: 'Wake up, Blenny dear, we must discuss the invitations to our dinner-party.'

'I am rather sleepy,' said he, 'but read the list over to me.'

Mrs. B. read the names of Mr. Tan-Terrier, Mr. Foxhound, Mr. Dane, Mr. Mastiff, Mr. Beagle, Mr. Poodle, Mr. Barker, Mr. Bulldog. 'Mr. Bulldog!' cried Mrs. B., looking vexed. 'Why do you ask him? No one considers him respectable.'

'It will not do to leave him out, dear!' said Mr. Blenheim, who then got up, and went lazily to the desk to write the invitations.

Pug, the page, went to Kennel Court, the country box of Mr. Foxhound, and found that sporting gentleman near home, wiping his brow after a good hunt. His manners were more blunt than his teeth, and his loud voice could be heard miles off. He was called a 'jolly dog', and seldom dined alone. But his great delight was the chase of a fox; he could then hardly give tongue enough to express his joy. After asking Pug after Mrs. Blenheim's health, he accepted the invitation.

Florio, the courier, waited on Mr. Barker with his invitation. Mr. Barker lived in a snug little house, in a farmyard, where he had the charge of watching over and protecting the live stock. He at first feared he must decline the invitation, but, on second thoughts, he resolved to go; it was not a late dinner, and he would manage to get away early. Unluckily, his coat was rather the worse for wear, but he could boast of a handsome collar at any rate – and so he accepted.

When Pug, the page, reached the dwelling-place of Mr. Bulldog, he found him lying in a dirty yard, smoking a short pipe very coolly. Mr. Bulldog snarled a little at being disturbed, and then read the invitation. 'Oh, you can say I'll be sure to come,' said he; 'I am always ready for a good feed. Now, young one,' said he to Pug, with a growl, 'I advise you to cut away as fast as you can!'

At last the day of the grand dinner-party arrived, and the guests all assembled, in good spirits, with keen appetites for the feast. Never had so many sleek, well-dressed dogs met together before, and the variety of their coats and countenances was very striking. All were, in respect for the gentle hostess, Mrs. Blenheim, on their best behaviour, and a friendly and happy atmosphere prevailed. Ample justice, too, was done to the good things liberally provided for the entertainment, and, strange to say for so large a party and so mixed a company, no excess was committed either in eating

or drinking. Social chat was the order of the day; compliments were exchanged, toasts, praising every guest in turn, were proposed and received with cordiality; speeches were made, which were applauded even when not called for or understood and for a long while it seemed that no Lord Mayor's feast could have passed off more brilliantly, or have given greater satisfaction.

Mr. Bulldog was, however, missing from among the guests after a time; it seems that he found the speeches rather dull, and so had sneaked off. Presently a great uproar was heard, and it was found that he had gone below, and had eaten up all the servants' dinner, so they had all joined together to punish him, and, after some trouble, contrived to kick him out of the house. And, very foolish he looked, in spite of his tipsy swagger.

As Mr. Bulldog had lost his pipe in the street, he thought he would turn into a public-house to get another. Here he again misbehaved, and was soon turned out; some mischievous boys then got hold of him, tied an old tin saucepan to his tail, and chased him through the streets. The faster he ran, the more he bumped himself with the saucepan. And the more he yelled with pain, the more the boys pelted him with mud and stones. At length he reached his dirty dwelling, more dead than alive. Poor Mrs. Blenheim! she was, indeed, much to be pitied, to have the nice dinner-party disturbed by so vulgar a creature. This shows how careful we should always be in avoiding low company.

A story without words

# THE ALPHABET OF GOODY TWO SHOES

A, was an Apple,
  And put in a pie,
With ten or twelve others,
  All piled up so high.

B, was tall Biddy,
  Who made the puff paste,
And put sugar and lemon-peel
  Quite to my taste.

C, is a Cheese,
  But don't ask for a slice,
For it serves to maintain
  A whole nation of Mice.

D, was Dick Dump,
  Who did nothing but eat,
And would leave book and play,
  For a nice bit of meat.

E, is an Egg,
  In a basket with more,
Which Jimmy will sell
  For a shilling a score.

F, was a Forester,
  Dressed all in green,
With a Cap of fine fur,
  Like a King or a Queen.

G, was a Greyhound,
  As swift as the wind;
In the race of the course
  Left all others behind.

H, was a Hoyden;
  Not like you, nor like me;
For she tumbled about
  Like the waves of the sea.

I, was the ice
  On which William would skate;
So up went his heels,
  And down went his pate.

J, was Joe Jenkins,
  Who play'd on the fiddle,
And began twenty tunes,
  But left off in the middle.

K, was a Kitten,
  Who jump'd at a cork,
And learn't to eat mice
  Without plate, knife, or fork.

L, was a Lady,
  Who made him so wise;
But he tore her long train,
  And she cried out her eyes.

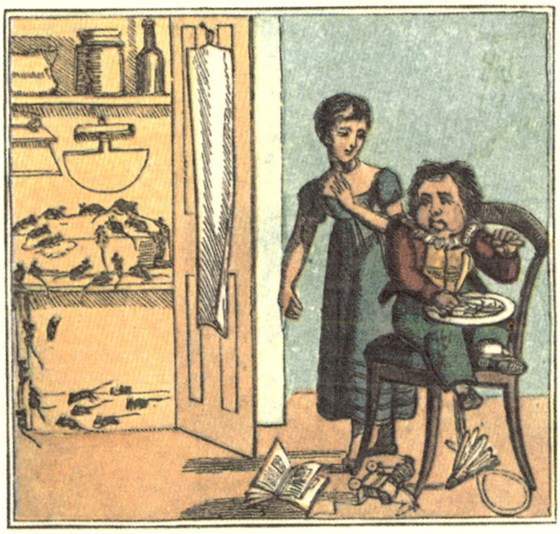

M, was Miss Mira,
Who turn'd in her toes,
And poked down her head,
Till her knees met her nose.

And N, Mr. Nobody,
Just come from France;
Said he'd set her upright,
And teach her to dance.

O, a grave owl:
To look like him, Tom tried;
So he put on a mask,
And sat down by his side.

P, was a pilgrim,
With a staff in his hand,
Return'd weary and faint
From a far distant land.

Q, was the Queen
Of Spades, I've heard say,
In her black velvet girdle,
Just dress'd for the play.

Here's Ralph with the Raree-show,
Calling so loud;
But I'd rather give two-pence
To look at the crowd.

And, U, an Umbrella
Saved Bell t'other day
From a shower that fell,
Whilst she turn'd the new hay.

V, was a Village,
Where lived near the brook
The renown'd Goody Two Shoes,
Who sends you this Book.

W, was a Witch,
Who set off at noon
To visit her cousin,
The Man in the Moon.

X, was Xantippe,
As you've heard before;
But, not to forget her,
I name her once more.

Y, was a youth,
Who walked in the Park,
And play'd on the Flute,
Till he made the Dogs bark.

Z, was a Zealander,
Whose name was Van Bley;
So here ends my song,
And I wish you Good-day.

# The tale of the four little mice

*Four little mice and their mother*
*Lived happily in their hole.*
*They had lots of food from the cellar*
*To satisfy body and soul.*

*But oh, those bad little creatures,*
*Were bored with their life underground,*
*They all thought that they'd like to travel,*
*That adventures were there to be found.*

*So when their Mama, one fine morning,*
*Was chatting with old Mrs Brown,*
*The mice bade farewell to the mouse hole,*
*And took themselves off towards town.*

*How splendid they found their new freedom,*
*How warm were the rays from the sun,*
*They hurried along feeling happy,*
*Expecting a life full of fun.*

*And at last when they felt tired and hungry,*
*Having travelled for most of the day,*
*It was but a very small matter*
*To decide where they all ought to stay.*

*But just like most little children,*
*When tired and needing a rest,*
*The mice soon started to quarrel,*
*Each certain that he knew best.*

*The first one sought a fine dwelling*
*Where someone he knew kept a shop,*
*And he thought himself very lucky*
*To find such a nice place to stop.*

*But the shopkeeper was not so stupid.*
*The mouse had no chance of a nap.*
*Before he had found a quiet corner,*
*Our young friend was caught in a trap!*

*The second one thought he was clever,*
*And went to a warm baker's shop,*
*Where he found bread and grain in abundance,*
*And ate till he thought he would pop.*

*But the moment the baker first noticed*
*What the small furry person was at,*
*He very soon made it his business*
*To point the mouse out to his cat.*

*The third of our four mice, so foolish,*
*Stole from an old lady – for shame!*
*She soon saw her food had been nibbled,*
*And cried out, 'Now who is to blame?'*

*So then the old lady decided*
*That she'd catch the bad little thief.*
*She prepared a mouse meal full of poison,*
*And the naughty brown mouse came to grief.*

*But what was the fate of the fourth mouse,*
*Who roamed round the town all alone ?*
*He thought of his poor lonely mother*
*And decided to journey back home.*

*How pleased was his mother that evening,*
*When her child scuttled in through the door*
*She took him and hugged him so closely,*
*He swore he would leave home no more.*

Darling kitten

# Whittington and his cat

Who has not heard of Whittington,
Thrice Lord Mayor of London Town?
In former times, (for long ago
Lived Whittington, as records show,)
Poor country lads were often told
That London streets were paved with gold.
One day, as Dick upon the grass
Reclined, a waggon chanced to pass
To London Bound: this thought occurr'd –
I'll see if all is true I've heard:
So jumping up, away he ran,
1. And walk'd beside the waggon-man.
Judge Richard's feelings of surprise,
When London really met his eyes!
Not yet by sad experience taught,
His mind was fix'd in pleasing thought.
His friend the waggoner pass'd on;
Poor Whittington was left alone;
That night was houseless. In the morn,
The youthful wanderer rose forlorn:
Exhausted, spiritless and faint,
The poor lad utter'd no complaint;
But, weeping, stretch'd himself before
A wealthy Merchant's open door.
The portly Cook, who lived at ease
And slighted Richard's miseries,
Bade him depart, with angry face,
And seek another resting place.
Just at this moment to his home
The worthy master chanced to come:
2. 'Why lie you there, my lad?' said he,
'Labour you do not like, I see.'
'I never would,' was Dick's reply,
'Thus idly on your door-steps lie,
Could I but work obtain, I'm weak,
And vainly for employment seek.'
'Get up, poor fellow; let me see –
Go, help them in the scullery.'
Soon as the morning sun arose,
Dick quickly to the kitchen goes
To ply his task; and though the Cook
Oft greeted him with sullen look,
He still determined to obey,
And sought to please her every way.
Yet still she scolded, still would try
To make him from her service fly;
Nay more, she sometimes took a broom,
3. And beat poor Richard round the room;
But Whittington, as Christian should,
Always requited ill with good.
Within the room where Richard slept,
The rats and mice a revel kept;
And nightly as he lay in bed,
They ran across his face and head:
Among such plagues the attempt was vain
Refreshing sleep or rest to gain.
Yet patient Dick did not repine,
He made his master's slippers shine.
The merchant's eye his labour traced:
And finding kindness rightly placed,
Sent him a penny by the maid, –
Industry always is repaid.
4. With this poor Richard bought a Cat,
Dire enemy to mouse and rat.
Puss went to work that very night,
5. And put the rats and mice to flight.
The Merchant had an only child,
A daughter affable and mild,
6. From whom poor Richard learn'd to read.
Slowly indeed did he proceed;
But those who readily pursue
The proper path, may wonders do.
Just like the snail, which seldom fails
To reach the top of garden-rails,
Because with diligence its race
Continues till it gains the place.
The merchant summon'd to the hall
His clerks and servants, one and all,
Told of his Ship, and then explain'd
How wealth was by her cargo gain'd;
To fill the white and spreading sail,
His Captain waited for a gale;
Then ask'd if each would like to send
Something which might to profit tend.

1

2

3

4

5

6

All but young Richard heard with joy
This kind proposal; he, poor boy!
Stood mute and mournful. 'Why so sad?
Hast nothing for a venture, lad?'
'No, Sir,' in downcast tone he said,–
'Only a Cat, Sir, over-head.'

7. 'Well, bring the Cat, my lad; let's see
How fortunate poor Puss may be.'
Dick wept his tabby friend to lose;
His grief served others to amuse.
All ask'd him if his famous Cat
Would catch a fine gold mouse or rat?
Or whether for enough 'twould sell
To buy a stick to beat him well?
At last poor Richard's temper fail'd,
And anger for a time prevail'd:
For all he did or tried to do,
Still worse and worse Cook's conduct grew.
Darkness had scarcely pass'd away,
On the morning of All-Hallows day,
When from the house he turn'd to go
With heavy heart and footsteps slow.
His future path unknown, he sigh'd;
For all was new and yet untried.
To Holloway he walk'd, when, lo!
He heard the merry bells of Bow:
In Richard's ear they seem'd to chime
This uncouth, strange, and simple rhyme:

8. 'Turn again, Whittington,
'Thrice Lord Mayor of London.'
Mayor of London!–can there be
Such honour yet design'd for me?
To London Dick return'd before
His tyrant oped the kitchen door.
The Merchant's ship, by weather tost,
Was driven on the Barbary Coast.
The Monarch of that distant land
Had hourly visits from a band
Of puny thieves–even rats and mice,
Who ate up all things sweet and nice.
The Captain offer'd Dicky's Cat,

9. Which snapp'd up every mouse and rat.
'Now,' said the King, 'cost what it may,
That creature must not go away,
But for the Cat I'll give you more
Than for the rest of all your store.'
And so he did; and bags of gold
Upon the carpet they behold.
Which quickly to the ship convey'd
Most nobly for poor Pussy paid.
The Captain back to England came,
The herald of Dick's wealth and fame.
I need not say, to all he'd send
To share his wealth, to all a friend.
The cross Cook even was not forgot,
Now Heaven had so improved his lot;
And numbers bless'd the happy hour
Which gave poor Richard wealth and power.

10. The Merchant wishing Richard joy,
Said, 'May you, simple honest boy,
Be happy! May you ever be
Famed for your strict integrity!'
Sheriff of London he was made,
And in his new career display'd
Manners so mild yet dignified,
So free from forwardness and pride,
That all the Corporation said
He must an Alderman be made.
In this high office praise he earn'd,
And shortly after was return'd
Lord Mayor of London: then he told
What once he thought the bells foretold.
He thrice the Civic honour gain'd,
And each time general praise obtain'd.
When the heroic Henry came
Fresh from the well-fought field of fame,
In City chronicles we find,
With Whittington the Monarch dined.

11. The gentle Emma now became
A blooming bride to grace his name,
To bless his fireside hours, and share
The honours of the great Lord Mayor.
Let every Child who reads this tale,
Remember Virtue cannot fail
To be beloved: that Wealth cannot
Confer true glory on our lot;
And that respect and love outweigh
The idle pleasures of a day:
That none on poverty should frown,
Nor on an honest man look down,
Since every virtue may adorn
The being whom you treat with scorn,
And none to wealth or rank can say,
'Ye cannot, shall not flee away.'
To make his glory yet more bright,

12. Our Whittington was dubb'd a Knight.
Sir Richard fully understood
The pure delight of doing good;
Rejoiced to succour the oppress'd,
And aid the humble and distress'd
A life in constant virtue spent,
Became his proudest monument.

7

10

8

11

9

12

The first time on roller skates...

The bold fire brigade

Blossoming spring

# THE CHERRY TREE

Three little sisters sat to supper
And though they'd had their fill,
The maid brought second helpings
To tempt the strongest will.

'Dear Auntie,' said our Katie,
'What makes the tart so nice?'
But Auntie said, 'A minute please,
Be patient for a trice!'

The little girls thus waited,
As quiet and still as mice,
Till Auntie said, 'I'll tell you now,
It's cherries give the spice.'

Then cried the mother, 'Darlings!
Don't swallow one stone more,
For otherwise, my little ones,
There's tummy-ache in store.'

Now Kate and Suzie gladly
Did what their mother said,
But not so little Vicky, who
Some twenty cherries had.

Then Suzie, Kate and Vicky
Went back to play again,
But alas, it wasn't long
'Ere Vicky felt a pain.

The pain got worse and even worse,
Till morning, at cock-crow,
Oh darlings, there from Vicky's mouth
A tree began to grow.

A cherry tree it was that grew,
And juicy fruit did bear,
But a nymph among the branches
Spoke these words for all to hear.

'Oh you who may be given
Such fruit as this to eat,
Know Vicky all her lifetime, will
Her foolishness regret.'

Poor Vicky wept, to no avail;
Yet faster grew the tree.
So you who like your cherries,
Remember well that tree!

# Little bear

So my dearest little bear,
No supper least, not yet!
Long way past your bedtime too.
Oh, how could I forget?

Sitting there so patiently;
But supper's nearly ready.
Come along my little chap,
Sweet spoonfuls for my Teddy.

One, two, three – and off to bed.
Bedclothes warm to make you.
When it's time for getting up,
Mummy comes to wake you.

Like bugs in a rug lay three children
But when called by the clock's waking ring
From their warm beds they leap,
Dress, and wash off the sleep!
What a bright early morning, they sing!

One quickly gets on with her dressing,
The next scrubs her cheeks all a'glow
Whilst she sings like a bird;
Oh, but not so the third –
She's a lazy young lady, I've heard!

Dora has today some callers,
Little Suzie, Jean and May;
She's the mother, whilst young Lottie
Opens up the shop today.

May and Suzie start their shopping –
See what Jeannie's up to now,
Her pinny slips with buttons popping –
A splendid ladies' train, I'll vow.

Sister dear, I've come to call.
See, the apple I have brought you.
I come in quietly on tiptoe,
Just like Mother said I ought to.

Shall I fetch the puppet theatre?
Spread it out upon your bed.
Here are Seven Dwarfs and Snow White—
But first the pillows; lift your head.

'Tell me where you journey, pray?
Captain, may I travel too?
Any cabin space will do.'
'Room for one there is, this day
Come aboard without delay.'

'Step upon the deck with care.
Stand by! Now we're casting off
Hoist with care the sail aloft
Then to the cabin you repair
To rest awhile. The weather bodes fair.'

On every beach in a faraway land,
  Stands a tall wicker-basket chair.
It keeps off the chills
  And all manner of ills,
Giving shade to the skin and fair hair.

If blown by the wind to lie flat on the sand,
  It's no longer a basket chair.
But a fisherman's boat
  And we voyage afloat
With a sail to the breeze blowing fair.

*We have no more bread for you!*

# The Childhood of Queen Wilhelmina

[One rainy Wednesday afternoon, a mother was telling her five children, John, James, Jill, Thomas and Susan, about Princess Wilhelmina, who became Queen of The Netherlands (1898–1948)]

'We are at the palace near Apeldoorn, the lovely country residence of the Royal Family. It is seven o'clock on a summer's morning. The sun is shining through the windows of the large bedroom and it wakes with a kiss the two blue eyes that have been closed for the whole night behind the white curtains of a lovely cot. Our princess gets up, and washes and dresses. She has breakfast with her parents and straight away begins the first of her lessons for the day...'

'Does she go to school?' Jilly interrupted.

'No, it is just not done for children of the Royal Family to go to school. I'm sure that the little princess would very much like to sit under the same roof as a lot of other children, to take the same lessons and to think up the same games together. But she cannot really do all these things. Little princesses always have their lessons on their own. Clever teachers come to teach her something about everything, every day.

'She must of course learn everything and that means subjects that you children haven't even thought of yet. For our princess must become a very clever queen. When the time comes for her ministers to come to her with talk about governing the country, then she must know all about what is going on in the world.

'Our dear little princess, who is still able to play undisturbed, shall in time have to know all that is necessary in the ruling of a kingdom. She will have to be aware of everything that is going on in her country, about the army, the navy and the possessions overseas. That is why she has so much to learn and must study hard.

Her teachers see to it that she becomes wiser and more clever as the days pass by. But the best of all the lessons are those learned at her mother's knee; her mother's words remain engraved upon her heart, and make her good and loveable.'

'When the King was still in good health, our little princess spent hours every day with her father, King William III. But everyone knew how very ill His Majesty was in the last years of his life which were spent in the sheltered sick room. So it was that Queen Emma had to be at once father and mother to the princess.

'In her "chalet", a Swiss-style house in the middle of the palace grounds, are the playrooms of the princess where she goes every day. But first, accom-

panied by her dog, Swell, the princess goes to feed the doves. A great flapping of wings fills the air. The doves have seen her, with her little basket full of seeds and come flying straight to her. Swell is used to being slapped about the ears by the doves' wings and accepts it with patience! He looks up in amazement at the way his young mistress spreads the food over the ground with such grace whilst surrounded by birds, flapping their wings and cooing.

'Let us just peep into the chalet. Oh, if I could but tell you about all the beautiful toys in there, I would need days and days! The princess has a large rocking horse, but she seldom rides it now that she can ride a proper horse – her little pony.'

'How many dolls does she have?' asked Jilly.

'Too many to count; certainly over thirty. You can just imagine how busy the princess is with them all! So she has a farmer's wife doll to help her with her busy housekeeping. Because dolls are as dumb and as ignorant as children, the little princess teaches them everything that she has learnt in her own lessons. Amongst the dolls is one boy who gives her a lot of trouble. At her wit's end, the princess eventually threatens him.

'"Now look here, my patience is at an end. If you cannot behave yourself better, I shall never make you an officer, nor shall I let you join the navy – understand? Why do you not take example from the other dolls? As reward for their good behaviour, several have been promoted to officer and sent off to fight in our colonies!"

'You must all have a look at the princess's sweet little cupboards, full of lovely tidy dolls' clothes, and dolls' furniture – beds, cots, wash-tables, dinner and tea services, silver and crystal; everything is the best that can be had.'

'But, Mamma, is the princess always on her own?' asked Suzy, stealing a glance at her brothers and sisters and thinking how dreary it would be at home without all those naughty faces around!

'She is often on her own. It could hardly be otherwise for an only child, but other children do often come to visit her. Then there is leaping and dancing with cries and shouts under the majestic trees in the old park. When the princess has her birthday, everything is done to make sure that the children have as good a time as possible. They enjoy riding in the beautiful boats most. They are rowed through the mirror-smooth water, and swans swim along gracefully and slowly, curious to look closer at all these happy young people.'

'The little princess has six ponies. Four of them are often harnessed to her little pony-cart. I wish you could all see the clever way these ponies know just what to do!'

Very soon after this conversation between mother and children, the ageing King William III passed away. All Holland went into mourning, and the little princess lost her beloved father. The little princess became Queen.

# The Cuckoo

*Cuckoo,*
*cuckoo,*
*whisper my*
*little one*
*a song*
*of birds,*
*of*
*sweet*
*spring flowers*
*and sun.*

# *The talking bird or Dame Trudge and her parrot*

INTRODUCTION

Of old Goody Trudge and her talkative bird,
My juvenile friends may have probably heard,
Or seen some account of at least:
But lest you should not, I'll attempt in my verse,
Her whimsical oddities now to rehearse;
For sure they'll afford you a feast.

THE GIFT

Dame Trudge had a brother, a rover was he,
Who quitted his country, fam'd India to see;
And on his return he thus sung:
'Think not, my dear sister, I'm laden with pelf,
But thank your kind stars that I've brought back myself,
And brought you a bird with a *tongue.*'

THANKS

'O lovely! O charming!' his sister exclaim'd,
'I've often been told the East Indies were fam'd
For birds that could chatter and sing:
My brother! you now have approv'd yourself kind,
For this is a gift so exact to my mind,
'Tis just the identical thing.'

THE PROMISE

1. Now Old Goody Trudge with her parrot began
To lay down a simple, but excellent plan,
By which they might still be together:
'Whene'er,' said the dame, 'I on visiting go,
Perch'd safe on my shoulder, my Poll shall go too,
Provided it be not bad weather.'

PREPARATIONS FOR VISITING

The promise was made with a view to be kept:
The dame and her parrot both heartily slept,
And soon in the morning awoke.
'Today,' said the Goody, 'my Poll shall take tea
With old neighbour All-gossip, where we shall see
Or hear of some subject for joke.'

ARRIVAL AT MISS ALL-GOSSIP'S

The swift circling moments flew merrily round;
The visitors went—and a parrot they found
On the top of Miss All-gossip's head.
Dame Trudge paid her compliments, sat herself down
Her parrot flew up to the side of her crown,
And listen'd to all that was said.

SCANDAL

Miss All-gossip talk'd, to be sure, as her tongue
Had been upon wires most tastefully hung,
And freely anointed with oil;
The *ladies* afforded her ample employ—
She cut up their persons and dresses with joy,
And cruelly laugh'd o'er the spoil

DANGER OF BEING TALKATIVE

2. 'My dear!' said our Poll to Miss All-gossip's bird,
'Pray tell me, if ever so much you have heard
Of your mistress, what *gentlemen* say?'
'A *Venus!*' the humorous creature replied—
'Aye, aye' said the other; 'but truth may be tried,
When *beauty* shall vanish away.'

OFFENCE

A wound may be given, though aim'd in the dark—
Miss All-gossip felt the intended remark;
She knew she to *fibbing* was prone:—
Her countenance fell, and her anger was fir'd,
The tea was remov'd, and the guests soon retir'd,
To leave the poor lady alone.

DANCING

3. A few days elaps'd, Goody Trudge was amaz'd,
And, trust me, young reader, as equally pleas'd,
When Puss and her parrot she found
A minuet performing with excellent grace,
Which—had it but been in a suitable place—
With shouts of applause had been crown'd.

A CONCERT

4. A dance and a concert were afterwards plann'd,
Puss play'd on the fiddle, though not with a hand,
She did quite as well with her paw:
Poll sung by the notes, while Pug on the ground,
Both footed with spirit and turn'd himself round,
As neatly as ever you saw.

QUARRELLING

5. But after this sport, a sad quarrel occurr'd
Between Goody's magpie, and Poll, her best bird,
Which caus'd much ill language and rage:
The old lady's temper was now so much try'd,
She scolded them both, and she beat them beside,
And fasten'd them each in their cage.

SYMPTOMS OF GOOD CONDUCT

6. The punishment over, and pardon receiv'd,
Our parrot contriv'd her good name to retrieve,
By reading, when weather prov'd wet,
A lecture on heads, replete with true fun;
Then next, as a governess, school she begun,
7. And read to her Dame the Gazette.

1

4

2

5

3

6

SACRE-JAFF
7

10

FRANCE
8

2
D. TRUDGE
Life of Tam Thumb
CAUSE between PUG & PUSS
11

9

12

### FURTHER ECCENTRICITIES

8. Dame Trudge's militia this parrot review'd,
And (hiding her mistress's work) she pursu'd
A plan she had form'd by the bye:—
The fortunes of all her companions she told,
How some should be punish'd for being too bold,
And some should old bachelors die.

### DISASTER AT MARKET

9. When Poll, Pug and Puss, Squirrel, Mag, and the Dame,
In solemn procession to market all came;
It sure was a laughable sight!

10. But when the great dog made his dreadful attack,
And a quarrel ensu'd as the party came back,
O there was a terrible fight!

### POLL TURNED COUNSELLOR

11. Victorious at length, and return'd from the town,
See Poll, in her counsellor's wig, band, and gown,
Most solemnly reading a brief!
But sorry I am my young readers to tell,
That Poll, who could read and could argue so well,
Should at last prove a bit of a thief.

### INGRATITUDE

12. 'Tis shocking, most shocking, but surely too true—
Away with her Goody's best bonnet she flew,
Nor could be persuaded to stop.
If by chance her adventures should ere come to light,
The whole of the tale I'll immediately write,
And you'll get it at HARRIS's shop.

## *Dinner party of the animals*

Rescued

# Rescued

*Our Dolly is allowed to bathe,*
*It's healthy, clean and sound*
*To paddle through the briny wave*
*Like Nero, our old hound.*

*But, how cross are all the seabirds,*
*Squawking as they fly!*
*Why do they have to send such words*
*A'screaming through the sky?*

*The doll, afraid, tripped over*
*And fell flat in the sea;*
*Her cries were heard to Dover*
*As she floated far from me.*

*But Nero saw the danger dire—*
*Her fate beyond all doubt—*
*And just before the end was nigh,*
*The good dog fished her out.*

# Well trained

*A trio of doggies has Ada,*
*Trained to a high degree.*
*On straight hind legs they stride about,*
*So clever for all to see.*

*At breakfast times, Miss Ada*
*Would save a chunk of bread,*
*And with patience her bright young puppies*
*Look forward to being fed.*

*When from Ada comes 'Up' the order,*
*Each in step with the others' feet,*
*They march to their happy young mistress,*
*Each one to enjoy his treat.*

## At the wash-tub

Here comes Johnny, clothes and feet
Wet and muddy from the street.
Good that mother's out just now –
She'd be awfully cross, I vow!
So his sister, deft and quick
Takes his clothing
for
a
wash

In the great big yellow bathtub,
Soft, warm water – splish, splash, splosh.

# The story of greedy Fred

An unassuaged sweet tooth had Fred.
He'd spurn his cabbage, wholemeal bread;
To rich concoctions he would turn.
For chocolates and for sweets he'd yearn.
The wretched boy was wont to fish
In every palatable dish
That by the maid was left behind,
And he would eat what he could find.
On this occasion, like a dream,
Was left behind a pot of cream.

Thus knelt young Frederick on a chair
Whilst Ermintrude, the cat, stood near.
He raised the cream-pot to his lips,
But the maid entered, hands on hips;
Surprised, Fred sipped, but spilled the rest
Down knickers, socks and fancy vest.
So there, all white with cream a'dripping,
Stood Fred whilst hoots and shrieks came ripping
Through open door, where all the others—
Sisters, cousins, friends and brothers—
Stood to call him 'Greedy-guts'
And 'Rumble-tum' and names as such.
Fred looked about him with a sigh
But no more felt his greed come nigh.
The moral of this tale of Fred,
Is little more than I have said.
Young scavengers must plain be able
To abstain from filching from the table.

# The Tale of Naughty Charles

No creature could be free from Chas.
No dog, no cat, no long-eared ass.
He'd tweak small puppies by their tails
And widely grin to hear their wails.
No kitten would be free from he
Who'd change their milk to scalding tea.

But when he took to plague a horse
His foibles took a different course.

A splendid beast, one fateful day,
With rider 'up', a sturdy bay
Was horrified to find a hair
From out its tail was plucked, sans care.

Reaction came – a neigh, a bellow
And well-aimed hoof at plaguey fellow
Who fell, with lacerated skin
Where horse-shoe struck him on the shin.
Resolved Charles never, as he lay
In pain, no further tricks to play
On animals of any sort –
His lesson learned, but dearly bought.

# Dutch picturebooks 1800-1805

## THE STREET ORGAN WITH DANCING FIGURINES

Wandering, looked upon by the poor,
With an organ in the street.
He tries to keep the wolf from the door,
Working hard to make ends meet.
You can always see the rabble
Who assemble fancy free,
Open-mouthed to gape and gabble,
Dancing figures just to see.
Round and round each one is turning,
Like a dancer on its toes!
Some small coins are all he's earning,
Organ playing, off he goes.

## THE CHICKEN MARKET

'Who will buy some lovely chickens?'
Wonders Master Beakynose.
So it is, on Monday morning
He to a chicken market goes.
Tony Miller makes an offer
Beakynose just can't refuse;
Takes possession of six chickens,
A rooster too to crow the news.
All at once, a rush of trouble;
Rover and the rooster eye
One another with displeasure—
Boldly at each other fly!

## THE FLOWER MARKET

Mother Goodheart, once out walking,
Chanced to buy from Levie Ross
A pair, or so, of lovely pot plants
For her darling daughter, Floss.
Children should be just like flowers,
Try to grow up like them too.
As the flowers are rich in colours,
Children should be kind and true.
Grow and bloom, beloved children
As the flowers bloom in the spring,
Blessings you will know for ever
And to others, joy will bring.

## PICKING FLOWERS

The sisters, two, hear Jilly cry,
'Let's go picking flowers!
Mamma says the grass is dry
And we've no more work for hours.'
'Chain the daisies while we're talking!
Lot of nonsense, let me go!
I like scrapping more than walking,'
Naughty Pete says. 'Climbing, too!'
Jilly keeps a rein on brother.
She's afraid he'll have a fall.
Now she's plucking for her mother
The sweetest smelling blooms of all.

## THE BIRDS ON THE LEASH

Should you a lesson care to sample
And a pastime profit by,
Then dear children take example
From the birds who, leashed, you fly.
To tame the wayward creatures,
And their wanton movements rein,
From perch, through line to jesses,
Your will is well made plain.
So it is that wiser people
Fain would reckless youth restrain,
Ensuring children do as they ought to
And on virtue's path remain.

## THE FRUIT SHOP

The sweetest fruits they'd ever seen,
Pineapple and cantaloup,
Pears and apples, tangerine,
Piled up in a tempting group.
'If only Mother,' Bessie thought,
'Would buy some plums for us to eat.'
But Johnny said, 'I hope she's bought
some apples for our Sunday treat.'
This earth, by God is richly dressed
With love and goodness all around.
He has us with His fruits well blessed;
For everyone, His works abound.

# What befell Henry who was a tease

Now children all, who aim to please
And never stop to vex and tease,
Pray never ape this ne'er-do-well
Whose history I now must tell.

Henry was this pester's name,
This lad whose deeds were wont to shame
His parents from whose care he flew
Unkindly deeds the while to do.

So it was that he was able
To overturn the serving table
Of a grandam selling fruit
By swift uplifting of his boot.

Pears and apples to the ground
Fell with an awful sploshing sound
Whilst grandam dozing at her barrow
Woke with a shriek to freeze the marrow.

Swift to her aid came others, willing
To apprehend the little villain
Who, by the Law was roughly taken
Down to the gaol, his ego shaken.

Then in a cell, his fate to ponder,
He realised – and 'twas no wonder –
That those who tease can never please.
Thus do not you be one of these.

*Please, be careful!*

WHO'LL BUY?

*Sugar and spice and all that's nice*
*Everything at the lowest price.*

*Good morning, Ladies! will you try*
*My goods ? The best that you can buy.*

*Apples and pears are cheap today;*
*The plums are beauties I think you'll say.*

*But the customers thought the prices dear,*
*And the fruit not fine for the time of year.*

*The shopkeeper didn't sell much that day,*
*So he shut the shop and moved away.*

# The Children's Orchestra

# A STORY WITHOUT WORDS

# Welcome Old Longlegs

We've got some special news today
'The Storks are back,
they're back to stay!'
Oh, everyone is cracker-jack.

Outdoors at once, we three, let's go!
Our drums to rattle, trumpets blow
To welcome dear old Longlegs back.

*Learnt when young, when old, well done*

In Father's shoes

Let me see if Philip can
Be a little gentleman;
Let me see, if he is able
To sit still for once at table:
Thus Papa bade Phil behave;
And Mamma look'd very grave.

# The story of fidgety Philip

But fidgety Phil,
He won't sit still;
He wriggles
And giggles,
And then, I declare,
Swings backwards and forwards
And tilts up his chair,
Just like any rocking horse; –
'Philip! I am getting cross!'

See the naughty restless child
Growing still more rude and wild,
Till his chair falls over quite.
Philip screams with all his might,
Catches at the cloth, but then
That makes matters worse again.

Down upon the ground they fall,
Glasses, plates, knives, forks and all.
How Mamma did fret and frown,
When she saw them tumbling down
And Papa made such a face!
Philip is in sad disgrace.

Where is Philip, where is he?
Fairly cover'd up you see!
Cloth and all are lying on him;
He has pull'd down all upon him.
What a terrible to-do!
Dishes, glasses, snapped in two!

Here a knife, and there a fork!
Philip, this is cruel work.
Table all so bare, and ah!
Poor Papa, and poor Mamma
Look quite cross, and wonder how
They shall eat their dinner now!

*Sail, little boat!*

Agatha was a delightful child
And everyone loved her dearly.
With her pleasure in mind,
Her parents would find
The best for her birthday, yearly.

With her tenth anniversary due very soon
Her parents wanted to find
In the next week or two,
Without a to-do,
What gift was on Agatha's mind.

Thus a day or two later when Mother then said,
'It will soon be your birthday, of course.
So what shall we get
Our adorable pet?'
The young lady replied, 'Ma, a horse!'

'And yet, come to think of it, Mama,' she cried,
'It's' really a pony I need.
A pony to ride,
To saddle with pride
And to comb and to brush and to feed.'

When Agatha's birthday arrived at last,
Said Father, 'Now come along, Miss,
And with good effect,
Our present inspect
For then you will know what it is!'

Father and Agatha stablewards sped
To see her new pride in his stall.
Shining new leathers,
A glow on his withers
And a side-saddle too, to top all.

'Oh Father and Mother, what darlings you are!'
Said Agatha, holding Pa's arm.
'Please may Jacob, the groom,
Teach me, Pa, very soon,
So that off I may ride, without harm?'

Agatha's lessons were over quite soon,
So alone on the pony she flew
Over hill over dale,
Past the fields of spring kale,
And the spinney where primroses grew.

*Summer delight*

The funeral of the dead little bird

Come buy my cloth;
Cheap at the price.
Long-lasting colours—
No other as nice.

Lovely sweet oranges,
Red apples and green,
No better you'll buy,
No better you've seen.

I sell best glasses
For everyone's sight,
For old eyes and young eyes,
For day or for night.

Come buy my baskets
In reed or in cane,
For mothers, for children
And nobly-born dame

Buy a copper kettle,
An iron or a pot.
Have you any mending?
The tinker does the lot.

Milk for My Lady,
Fresh from the cow!
Weary am I from the yoke,
Let me rest now.

Would you like some potatoes,
Green peas or beans?
A lettuce or cabbage,
Or lovely spring greens?

Come buy my fine lace
It will ne'er tear or rent.
It comes not from Flanders
But from England's Kent.

Black pots for sale,
Teapot or jug,
A tea cup and saucer
Or strong heavy mug.

Mats for sale, mats for sale!
All that you need.
A mat for all uses
Of best Spanish reed.

Buy my lovely ornaments,
Nothing but the best.
For writing desk or table,
For mantelpiece or chest.

Scissors and knives
I sharpen and grind
With my wheel and my stone,
To a fine edge you'll find.

Who'll try my gherkins
In vinegar pickled?
Tasty and cheap
And your palate well tickled!

Buy my umbrellas
To keep off the rain,
A parasol too
When it's sunny again.

Old clothing, old clothing,
Old boots and old shoes.
Come, buy a bargain,
You've nothing to lose.

Come sisters, come look you
A lovely fresh fish.
Just see, he's still moving—
How lively he is!

Ready made shoes for sale,
Slippers and mules,
From Northampton craftsmen
And built to the rules.

Come buy my ripe cherries,
The best of all fruit.
Morellos or others,
Your own taste to suit.

The young girl liked a little box,
She just bought it from me,
But offered me too little
Till more we did agree.

Who'll buy my firewood?
None better than mine
To burn in your fireplace,
On damp days or fine.

*Wasn't it nice at the grocer's!*
*And what a lovely smell!*

The first snow

# THE SNOWMAN

The snowman wears
A white coat, thick,
And threatens with
A sturdy stick.
'You wouldn't dare!'
Shouts Pete. 'So there!'

First a snowball to be made,
A snowball pressed down hard;
'See now, its ready for the throw
He'll see I'm not afraid.
So here's a shot that he won't dodge,
The great fat podge!'

But, laughing, little Jill and Kate,
Who'd just come, hand in hand,
Called, 'His stick was shook by melting snow.
Let old Podge the snowman stand!'
And now it's time for them all to go
Back home to tea and fireside's glow.

*Joys of winter*

Even with a doll, it can be lonely

# Going to School

Soft and deep is still the snow
As we three off to school must go.

Cold finger tips and cold red nose –
But me, I'm tough, from head to toes!

# Dollies' teacher

With Granny's glasses on her nose,
And Granny's bonnet on her head;
Betty tries to teach her dolls
To understand the things she's read.

No answer from the biggest doll,
And next to her there's one asleep.
The smallest simply sits and stares.
Enough to make the teacher weep.

The difficult sum

# The story of the man that went out shooting

This is the man that shoots the hares;
This is the coat he always wears:
With game-bag, powder-horn and gun,
He's going out to have some fun.
The hare sits snug in leaves and grass,
And laughs to see the green man pass.
He finds it hard, without a pair
Of spectacles, to shoot the hare.
Now, as the sun grew very hot,
And he a heavy gun had got,
He lay down underneath a tree
And went to sleep, as you may see.
And, while he slept like any top,
The little hare came, hop, hop, hop,—
Took gun and spectacles, and then
On her hind legs went off again.

The green man wakes, and sees her place
The spectacles upon her face;
And now she's trying all she can,
To shoot the sleepy, green-coat man.
He cries and screams and runs away;
The hare runs after him all day
And hears him call out everywhere,
'Help! Fire! Help! The Hare! The Hare!'

At last he stumbled at the well. Head over ears, and in he fell.
The hare stopp'd short, took aim, and hark!
Bang went the gun,—she miss'd her mark!
The poor man's wife was drinking up
Her coffee in her coffee-cup;
The gun shot cup and saucer through;
'O dear!' cried she, 'what shall I do?'
There liv'd close by the cottage there
The hare's own child, the little hare;
But while she stood upon her toes,
The coffee fell and burn'd her nose.
'O dear!' she cried, with spoon in hand,
'Such fun I do not understand.'

What fun we have while haymaking!

# SIX IMPORTANT PROFESSIONS

THE BRICKLAYER PUTS BRICK UPON BRICK
WITH MORTAR, AND BUILDS A WALL.

THE CARPENTER USES WOOD TO MAKE CHESTS
AND OTHER PIECES OF FURNITURE.

THE STONEMASON CUTS BLOCKS OF STONE
TO THE SHAPE HE WANTS.

THE PAINTER USES HIS PAINTBRUSH TO PAINT
WHATEVER COLOUR IS WANTED.

THE BLACKSMITH SHAPES THE IRON
AT HIS ANVIL.

THE ENGINE DRIVER AND THE FIREMAN
MAKE THE ENGINE GO.

*Waving to the train*

# AN INVOLUNTARY SKY-RIDE

The aerial navigator, Kirsch, had announced the ascent of a huge air-balloon from the French town of Nantes. When the day arrived, a great crowd assembled to witness the event. Just when the balloon had been blown up, the ropes, secured to a strong stake in the ground, broke and the balloon began to rise. From the balloon there hung a rope with an anchor which was, at first, dragged along the ground. But suddenly the anchor locked itself firmly into the short trousers of a twelve-year-old boy, dragging him some distance over the ground, but causing him no injury. The young lad had the presence of mind to use his hands to steady himself by the anchor rope until, to the concern of the crowd, he was lifted high above the ground. A dreadful end seemed inevitable.

Later, the lad told of his feelings during his unexpected ascent toward the heavens. As soon as he be-

came aware of the dangerous situation in which he found himself, he uttered a short prayer and had then proceeded to shout at the top of his voice for help. He did not, fortunately, get dizzy and neither did he lose consciousness.

Looking beneath him, the boy became clearly aware of his predicament. He saw the crowd below as a seething column of ants and noticed that it followed the balloon. Resigning himself to his imminent departure from this life, he considered the likelihood of dropping upon a house or falling into the river Loire. He felt that a fall into water would, at least, be preferable to being dashed to pieces on the ground.

He floated higher still, but after a while he noticed that the balloon appeared to be shrinking and was on its way downwards. At this, he regained his courage and his hope; beginning the while to believe that rescue was at hand.

Approaching a haystack, he became aware of a number of people in the vicinity. 'Over here, friends!' he cried to them. 'Help me! Save me, or I am lost!'

Two men jumped up to him just before he touched the ground and one was able to catch him in his arms. The boy asked after his cousin who was living thereabouts and asked to be taken to him, rather than to his mother from whom he feared punishment!

The lad's health had in no way suffered during the fearful adventure, but his sleep became very disturbed. He dreamed, time and time again, of being carried by the balloon high up through the air and would cry out frequently for his mother's help. In the town of Nantes and the surrounding countryside, he was regarded as a hero, and so he was, of course, somewhat pleased and not a little proud!

*Saved from drowning*

# The story of cruel Frederick.

Here is cruel Frederick, see!
A horrid wicked boy was he;

He caught the flies, poor little things
And then tore off their tiny wings,

He kill'd the birds, and broke the chairs,
And threw the kitten down the stairs;

And Oh! far worse than all beside,
He whipp'd his Mary, till she cried.

# The story of cruel Frederick.

The trough was full, and faithful Tray
Came out to drink one sultry day;
He wag'd his tail, and wet his lip,
When cruel Fred snatch'd up a whip,

And whipp'd poor Tray till he was sore,
And kick'd and whipp'd him more and more,
At this, good Tray grew very red,
And growl'd and bit him till he bled;
Then you should only have been by,
To see how Fred did scream and cry!

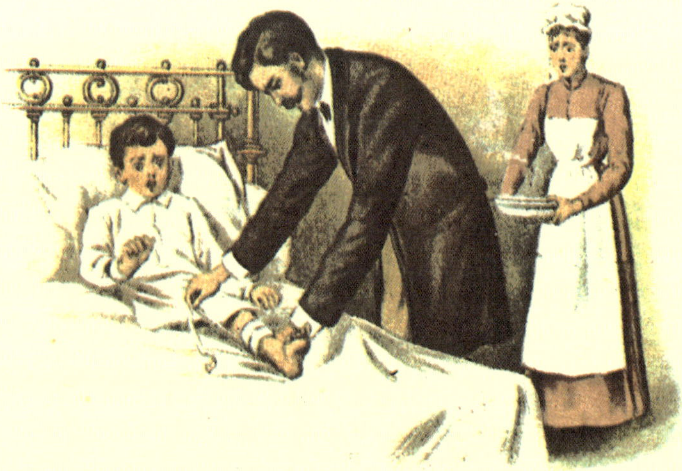

So Frederick had to go to bed;
His leg was very sore and red!
The Doctor came and shook his head,
And made a very great to-do,
And gave him nasty physic too.

But good dog Tray is happy now;
He has no time to say 'bow-wow!'
He seats himself in Frederick's chair,
And laughs to see the nice things there:
The soup he swallows, sup by sup, –
And eats the pies and puddings up.

*His best friend*

At the hairdresser's

# Shock-headed Peter

Just look at him! There he stands,
With his nasty hair and hands.
See! his nails are never cut;
They are grim'd as black as soot;
And the sloven, I declare,
Never once has comb'd his hair;
Anything to me is sweeter
Than to see Shock-headed Peter.

# The dreadful story about Harriet and the matches

It almost makes me cry to tell
What foolish Harriet befell.
Mamma and Nurse went out one day,
And left her all alone at play;
Now, on the table close at hand,
A box of matches chanc'd to stand;
And kind Mamma and Nurse had told her
That, if she touch'd them, they should scold her.
But Harriet said, 'Oh, what a pity!
For, when they burn, it is so pretty;
They crackle so, and spit, and flame;
Mamma, too, often does the same.'

The pussy-cats heard this,
And they began to hiss,
And stretch their claws,
And raise their paws;
'Me-ow,' they said, 'me-ow, me-o,
You'll burn to death, if you do so.'

But Harriet would not take advice,
She lit a match, it was so nice!
It crackled so, it burn'd so clear, —
Exactly like the picture here.
She jump'd for joy and ran about,
And was too pleas'd to put it out.

The pussy-cats saw this,
And said, 'Oh, naughty, naughty Miss!'
And stretch'd their claws,
And rais'd their paws;
''Tis very, very wrong, you know,
Me-ow, me-o, me-ow, me-o,
You will be burnt, if you do so.'

And see! Oh! what a dreadful thing!
The fire has caught her apron-string;
Her apron burns, her arms, her hair;
She burns all over, everywhere.

Then how the pussy-cats did mew,
What else, poor pussies, could they do?
They scream'd for help, 'twas all in vain!
So then, they said, 'we'll scream again;
Make haste, make haste, me-ow, me-o,
She'll burn to death, we told her so.'

So she was burnt, with all her clothes,
And arms, and hands, and eyes, and nose;
Till she had nothing more to lose
Except her little scarlet shoes;
And nothing else but these was found
Among her ashes on the ground.

And when the good cats sat beside
The smoking ashes, how they cried!
'Me-ow, me-oo, me-ow, me-oo,
What will Mamma and Nursy do?'
Their tears ran down their cheeks so fast;
They made a little pond at last.

# The story of Johnny Head-In-Air.

As he trudg'd along to school,
It was always Johnny's rule
To be looking at the sky
And the clouds that floated by.
Running just in Johnny's way,
Came a little dog one day.

Johnny's eyes were still astray
Up on high, in the sky;
And he never heard them cry—
'Johnny, mind, the dog is nigh!'
Bump! Dump!

Once with head as high as ever
Johnny walked beside the river.
Johnny watched the swallows trying
Which was cleverest at flying.

One step now, oh!
Sad to tell
Headlong in poor
Johnny fell.
And the fishes in
dismay
Wagged their tails and
swam away.

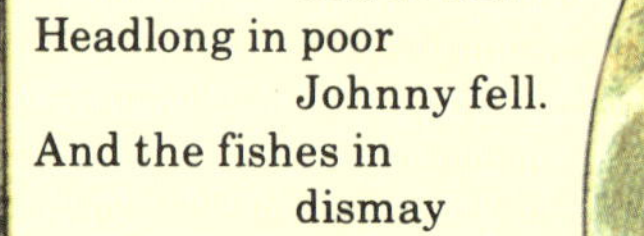

# The story of Johnny Head-In-Air.

There lay Johnny on his face,
With his nice red writing-case;
But, as they were passing by,
Two strong men had heard him cry;
And, with sticks, these two strong men
Hook'd poor Johnny out again.

Oh! you should have seen him shiver
When they pull'd him from the river.
He was in a sorry plight!
Dripping wet, and such a fright!

Wet all over, everywhere,
Clothes, and arms, and face, and hair:
Johnny never will forget
What it is to be so wet.

And the fishes, one, two, three,
Are come back again, you see;
Up they came the moment after,
To enjoy the fun and laughter.

Each popp'd out his little head,
And, to tease poor Johnny, said:
'Silly little Johnny, look,
You have lost your writing-book!'

# ROBBIE IS ILL

My lovely dog is feeling sickly;
The dripping from the larder's gone.
Now poor Robbie lies, unhappy,
Contemplating what he's done.

Come, my Robbie, here's some medicine
Drink some or in pain you'll lie.
Poor sad eyes are hardly open.
Robbie, dear, it makes me cry.

*High expectations*

# My dear pet lamb

My little lamb was, oh, so sweet,
  So clean and neat, so white;
But he paddled through the dirty mud
  To come out black as night!
I didn't want to know him then,
  Yet back to me he came.
And off I sent him, on his way,
  To think about his shame.
But there he stood, a'bleating
  So sadly and forlorn,
As if, poor thing, he said to me
  'Twas not my fault. Don't scorn.'

When May, our maid, first heard my lamb,
  She picked the beastie up,
And put him bleating loudly,
  Straight in the water tub.
When May began to wash him,
  As if he was a child,
The little creature lay so calm,
  So trusting, sweet and mild.
And then from out the water tub
  So white and clean he came,
Said I, 'Now you are just as sweet,
  My dearest, dear pet lamb!'

# At the pump

I'm not quite five years old yet.
I'm small, so very small,
But helping Mother round the house
Is what I like most of all.

And of the tasks that I do best,
The one I find most dear,
Is filling up the drinking jug
With water, fresh and clear.

# FATHER'S EYES

*My father sails the oceans.*
*I am a seaman's child,*
*And so I love the foamy sea*
*In weathers wild or mild.*
*So is it that I often*
*Stand near the harbour wall,*

*But run to say to Father,*
*'Can't see, I'm much too small!'*
*At that, if not too busy,*
*He'll lift me off my feet*
*To set me on a bollard—*
*My favourite viewing seat.*

*His telescope extended*
*Against my eager eye,*
*I scan the far horizon*
*And then a ship I spy.*
*But Dad's already seen it—*
*No telescope needs he;*

*At dusk, through miles of twilight,*
*He'll name a ship at sea.*
*He sees all sorts of secrets,*
*And this I know beside,*
*When he sometimes looks at me*
*And my eyes are opened wide*

*So deep he sees, he always learns*
*The vision of my heart.*
*Straight through he looks*
*As if to take my inmost thoughts apart.*
*And when his steady gaze I feel,*
*No naughtiness I'd dare,*

*But however long he looks at me,*
*I've not the littlest fear.*

# Ernest, who scribbled on walls

This tale relates to what befalls
Small boys who write on doors and walls.
Young Ernest was a terrible child.
When he saw wet paint he went quite wild!

Thus it was, some painting done,
Ernest thought he'd have some fun.
He saw a house bright red and white,
A house, fresh painted, gleaming bright.

Ernest ran to work his will;
As first he smudged the windowsill;
And then inscribed upon the door
The sum of two times two is four.

A painter, just refreshed with tea,
Was greatly horrified to see
His patient toil so foul besmirched,
And cried, 'The culprit should be birched!'

Instead, the painter, thinking fast,
A tin of paint and brush he grasped,
And striped the boy in bottle green
From head to toe with brilliant sheen.

The howls of mirth from lookers-on
Continued until all had gone;
And Ernest promised with a moan
All painted walls he'd leave alone.

# The woeful tale of Peter, who would clamber

A thoughtless lad was little Pete.
He cared not where he placed his feet,
Negotiating each arm-chair
Yet caring not for rent nor tear.

His gentle mother bad him, daily,
'Desist from clambering so gaily
Over every chair and table,
Which you think that you are able.'
She also tried to chide him, so,
'Who heedeth not, repenteth slow!'
His mother's word he did not heed,
But went on, his whim to feed.

Until one sunny afternoon
A window open, in his room,
Our climber clambered to the sill
To bite at last the bitter pill
In payment of his wayward wont;
His mother shouted, ‘Peter, don’t!’
Alas, too late. His mother saw
That Peter’s climbing days were o’er.

# Of Frank – a lazy boy

Of sleep, the lazy Francis had
So much, that most who knew the lad
Would call him, 'Lazy bones', whilst some
Would merely find him rather dumb.

Remarking on his girth, they'd mutter,
'This rounded youth is fat as butter!'
But then, you see, it was no use.
Poor, idle Frank, that silly goose.

It's drier here!

A welcome shelter from the rain

Nanny wakes the children up in the morning

She helps the children to get dressed and do their hair

Before going out for a walk with Nanny, the children give their mother a big hug

In the afternoon, they have great fun in the play-room

# THE KIND-HEARTED LITTLE BOY

Ernest was a good boy. In the picture you can see him with a huge black dog who is sitting up and begging for him. Would you like to know how he came to own such a lovely animal?

When Ernest was still very small, he saw this dog in the hands of some street urchins. It was then only a little puppy and far from being as nice as it is now. A couple of urchins had a cord tied about the neck of the little animal and were dragging him towards the water so as to drown him. The young Ernest pleaded for mercy for the puppy. He begged his mother to buy it.

Ernest washed the puppy. He combed it too and saw that it had enough to eat and drink. And so the pup grew from day to day until it became the lovely dog you see in the picture.

Because of everything that Ernest had done for him, the dog was very, very faithful. I shall tell you something of this fidelity. One day, Ernest rashly took himself off in a small boat to fetch a piece of board that was drifting in the middle of a river. As he approached the board and leaned over to pick it up, he lost his balance and the boat tipped up to pitch Ernest into the water. There he would have drowned had not the faithful hound seen what was happening.

The dog at once sprang into the water, grabbed his small master by his clothing and pushed him back to the bank. So he saved Ernest's life, just as Ernest had saved his when the urchins were about to drown him!

A look in the zoo

The magic of spring

On the grassy banks
Lambkins at their pranks;
Woolly sisters, woolly brothers
  Jumping off their feet
While their woolly mothers
  Watch by them and bleat.

If a pig wore a wig,
  What could we say?
Treat him as a gentleman,
  And say 'Good day.'

If his tail chanced to fail,
  What could we do?—
Send him to the tailoress
  To get one new.

Sing me a song—
  What shall I sing?—
Three merry sisters
  Dancing in a ring,
Light and fleet upon their feet
  As birds upon the wing.

Tell me a tale—
  What shall I tell?—
Two mournful sisters,
  And a tolling knell,
Tolling ding and tolling dong,
  Ding dong bell.

Mix a pancake,
Stir a pancake,
  Pop it in the pan;
Fry the pancake,
Toss the pancake,—
  Catch it if you can.

My baby has a mottled fist,
  My baby has a neck in creases;
My baby kisses and is kissed,
  For he's the very thing for kisses.

'I dreamt I caught a little owl.
  And the bird was blue—'
'But you may hunt for ever
  And not find such an one.'

'I dreamt I set a sunflower,
  And red as blood it grew—'
'But such a sunflower never
  Bloomed beneath the sun.'

## ANGELA'S BIRTH

Angela came to us out of the flowers,
God's little blossom that changed into ours.

Cloves for her fingers, and cloves for her toes.
Eyes from the succory, mouth from the rose,

Loveliness sprang from the sisterly stocks,
Daffodils gave her those yellowy locks.

Fairies that visit her constantly meet
Lilies and lavender making her sweet.

Cherry-pie, pansy, forget-me-not, musk,
Wake in her dawning and sleep in her dusk.

Angela came to us out of the flowers,
God's little blossom that changed into ours.

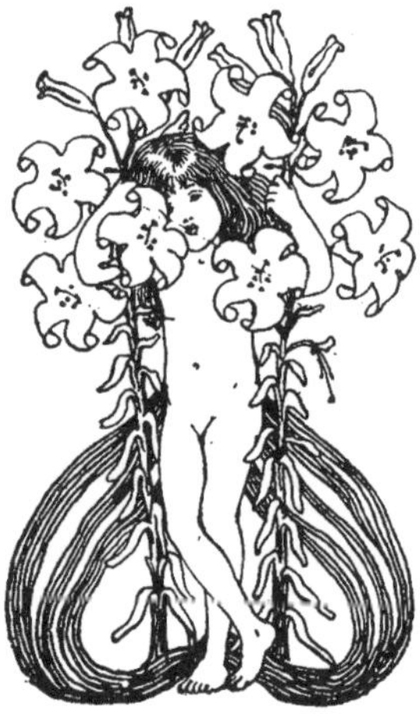

## TUBBING

Uncle Harry, hear the glee
Coming from the nursery!
Shall we just pop in to see
  Thomas in his tub?

In a soapy pond of joy,
Water as his only toy,
Sits my golden sailor-boy
  Thomas in his tub.

There he is, the little sweet,
Clutching at his rosy feet!
Make your toes and kisses meet,
  Thomas in the tub!

Partly come of fairy line,
Party human, part divine,
How I love this rogue of mine,
  Thomas in the tub!

*by Helen Stratton*

*by Kate Greenaway*

*by Kate Greenaway*

# *Shy Johnnie*

Uncle Tom and Aunt Kate came to visit us one day and brought with them our cousin John. We took him up to our room to find something with which to play. But, oh dear, what a strange boy he was! He sat down on a chair and acted as if he was a complete dim-wit. To anything we asked him, he would reply, 'I don't know.' At last we teased him by asking, 'But John, what *do* you know, then?' We thought it very funny when he answered, 'I don't know.' Who had ever met such a shy little chap?

Later on, we went to play in the garden and to fish out minnows with a net, from the pond. There, on the bank, Jill lost her balance and tumbled, all of a sudden, into the deepest part. 'Help, help! Jill's drowning,' we cried and went running off to the house. But just before Father, Mother, Uncle and Aunt had got to the pond, we saw that Shy Johnnie had jumped into the water and had got hold of Jill by her clothes.

So it was that Shy Johnnie who knew nothing, saved Jill's life, for without him she would certainly have drowned. From that day on, we no longer tried to make a fool of Johnnie, we became very, very fond of him and it became plain that he was not so shy after all, and he knew far more than we three little girls put together!

# ABROAD

WHILE chatting with Dennis, Rose lost all her fear;
And the swift Albert Victor came safe to the pier
At Boulogne, where they landed, and there was the train
In waiting to take up the travellers again.
But to travel so quickly was not their intent:
On a little refreshment our party was bent.
Here they are at the Buffet—for dinner they wait—
And the tall *garçon*, André, attends them in state.

At a separate table sits Monsieur Legros,
And behind him his poodle, Fidèle, you must know,
Who can dance, he's so clever, and stand on his head,
Or upon his nose balance a morsel of bread.
Mabel takes up some sugar to coax him, whilst Nell
Calls him to her—Fidèle understands very well—
'Why! he must have learnt English, he knows what we say,'
Mabel cries, 'See!—he begs in the cleverest way.'

THEN to the Hotel on the quay they all went;
To remain till the morrow they all were content:
After so much fatigue Father thought it was best,
For the children were weary and needed the rest.
Pictured here is the room in that very Hotel,
Where so cosily rested Rose, Mabel, and Nell.

Mabel dreamed of the morrow—of buying French toys:
Rose remembered the steam-pipe, and dreamed of its noise.
Nellie's dreams were of home, but she woke from her trance
Full of joy, just to think they were *really* in France.
Very early next morning, you see them all three
Looking out from their window that faces the sea.

*A visit to a French nursery school*

CHILDREN are happy with 'Sister' all day,
Mothers can't nurse them—they work far away.
Good Sister Rosalie, she is so kind,
E'en when they're troublesome, she doesn't mind.
Here in the first room the Babies we see, sitting at *déjeuner* round Rosalie.

Dodo is crying, he can't find his spoon—some one will find it and comfort him soon.
Over yon cradle bends kind Sister Claire,
Dear little Mimi is waking up there.
Sister Félicité, sweetly sings she,
'Up again, down again, *Bébé,* to me.'

# ARRIVAL AT CAEN

THROUGH Rouen when our friends had been,
And all its famous places seen,
They travelled on, old Caen to see,
Another town in Normandy.

Arrived at Caen, the travellers here
Before the chief Hotel appear,
Miss Earle, Rose, Bertie you descry—
The rest are coming by-and-by.

*Monsieur le Maître,* with scrape and bow,
Stands ready to receive them now.
And Madame with her blandest air,
And their alert *Commissionaire.*

NEXT up the staircase see them go,
With *femme de chambre* the way to show.
Father and Dennis, standing there,
Are asking for the bill of fare.

*Monsieur le Maître,* who rubs his hands
And says, 'What are *Monsieur's* commands?'
With scrape and bow, again you see—
The most polite of men is he.

HOTEL
E LA
ROYALE
SALLE à MANGER

# THE KNIFE-GRINDER OF CAEN

'L'HOMME qui passe,' in France they call
The man who thrives
By grinding knives—
Who never stays at home at all,

But always must be moving on.
He's glad to find
Some knives to grind,
But when they're finished he'll be gone.

With dog behind to turn the wheel,
He grinds the knife
For farmer's wife,
And pauses now the edge to feel:

The dog behind him hears the sound
Of cheerful chat
On this and that,
And fears no knife is being ground.

The man makes jokes with careless smile,
He doesn't mind
The dog behind,
But goes on talking all the while.

## CHOCOLATE AND MILK

LITTLE Lili, whose age isn't three years quite,
Went one day with Mamma for a long country walk,
Keeping up, all the time, such a chatter and talk
Of the trees, and the flowers, and the cows, brown and white.
Soon she asked for some cake, and some chocolate too,
For this was her favourite lunch every day—
'Dear child,' said Mamma, 'let me see—I dare say

'If I ask that nice milkmaid, and say it's for you,
Some sweet milk we can get from her pretty white cow.'
'I would rather have chocolate,' Lili averred.
Then Mamma said, 'Dear Lili, please don't be absurd;
My darling, you cannot have chocolate now:
You know we can't get it so far from the town.—
Come and stroke the white cow,—see, her coat's soft as silk.'
'But, Mamma,' Lili said, 'if the *White* cow gives milk,
Then chocolate surely must come from the *Brown.*'

FOR Paris quite an early start
They made the following day,
And out of windows every one
Kept looking, all the way.
And many a pretty road like this
The train went whizzing past,
Where gatekeeper, with flag and horn,
Stood by the gates shut fast.
That's Marie you see standing there:
Now, do you wonder why
A *woman* has to blow the horn
Before the train goes by?—
Her husband is a lazy man,
He's in his cottage near,
He would not stir a step, although
The train will soon be here.
And Marie called him, 'Paul, be quick—
Go shut the gate,' she cried—
'Don't hurry me, there's time enough,'
The lazy man replied.
So Marie had to go, you see,
And take the horn, and blow.—
And every day it's just the same,
She always has to go.

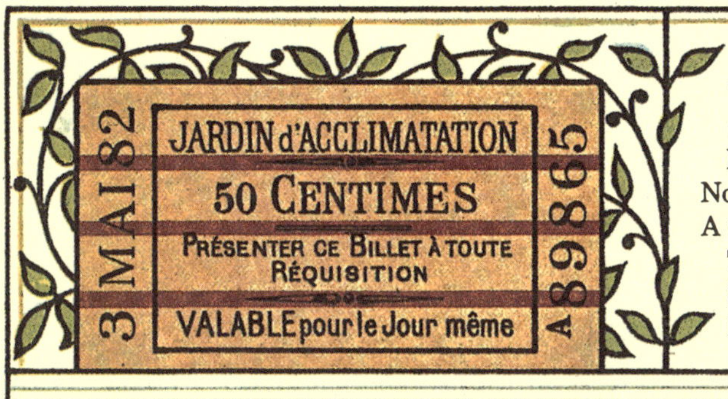


MUMBO and Jumbo, two elephants great,
From India travelled, and lived in state,
In Paris the one, and in London the other:
Now Mumbo and Jumbo were sister and brother.
A warm invitation to Jumbo came,
To cross the Atlantic and spread his fame.
Said he, 'I really don't want to go–
But then, they're so pressing!–I can't say No!'

So away to America Jumbo went,
But his sister Mumbo is quite content
To stay with the children of Paris, for she
Is as happy an elephant as could be:
'I've a capital house; quite large and airy,
Close by live the Ostrich and Dromedary,
And we see our young friends every day,' said she;
'Oh, where is the Zoo that would better suit me?'

PARIS, gay Paris! so bright and so fair,
Your sun is all smiles, and there's mirth in your air.

The children, though tired with their travelling, found
That the first night in Paris one's sleep is not sound,
For the hum of the streets makes one dream all the night
Of the wonderful sights that will come with the light.

The morning was fine, and—breakfast despatched—
They soon made their way to the Gardens attached
To the old Royal Palace, and there met a throng
Of French children, and joined in their games before long.

One boy lent his hoop, and gave Bertie a bun.
And—talking quite fast—seemed to think it great fun
With nice English girls like our Nellie to play,
Though not understanding a word she might say.

On leaving the Gardens, the party were seated
Outside of a *café*, and there Papa treated
Them all to fine ices and chocolate too;
They could hardly tell which was the nicer—could you?

Paris, gay Paris,
So bright and so fair!
Your sun is all smiles.
And there's mirth in your air!

ROSE and Bertie have a ride;
Mabel, walking at their side,
Carries both the dolls, and so
By the Luxembourg they go.

Over in that Palace soon—
For the clock is marking noon—
The 'Senate' will together come
(Like our 'House of Lords' at home).

## *IN THE LUXEMBOURG GARDENS*

Hear that woman, 'Who will buy
Windmill, ball, or butterfly'—
Josephine and Phillipe, see,
Eager as they both can be.

Charles befor her, silent stands,
With no money in his hands,
No more *sous*—he spent them all
On that big inflated ball.

Be content, my little friend,
Money spent you cannot spend;
With your good St. Bernard play,
Buy more toys another day.

NOW, with regret, they 've said Good-bye to Paris bright and gay;
To Calais they are drawing nigh—you see them on their way.
To travel thus, all through the night, at first they thought was fun.
But by degrees they grew less bright, as hours passed one by one.
Then Nellie to her sisters said, 'Let's have an extra rug,
And make-believe we're home in bed, and cuddle close and snug,
And try, until the night has passed, which can most quiet keep.'
Then all were tucked up warm and fast, and soon fell sound asleep.

The happy time abroad, again in dreams is all gone o'er—
Again in Paris, as it seems, they watch the crowd once more.
The 'Elysian Fields,' beneath the trees, are peopled with a throng
Of loveliest dolls, which at their ease converse, or ride along;
And wondrous 'Easter Eggs' in nests, abundant lie around,
And 'April Fish' with golden vests and silver coats, abound!
Such fleeting fancies Dreamland lends to pass the time away
Until the railway journey ends, just at the break of day.